Silence & Hope

Kelsey Santero

BookLeaf Publishing

India | USA | UK

Presentation by *BookLeaf Publishing*

Web: www.bookleafpub.com

E-mail: info@bookleafpub.com

ISBN: 9789360943073

First edition 2024

New Headquarters

To be loved is to be seen.
No one ever talks about how uncomfortable it
can be,
calm talks without judgment or screams,
without criticism and pointing out insecurities.

To be loved is to be heard.
Not interrupted or called a burden,
to lovingly hold you whenever you're hurting.
It isn't always easy to remember you're worth it.

You deserve all the love I pour
even when you feel like a mess,
and there's nothing you can do
to make me love you less.

The Close Between Us

I wish I could say we were still friends.
We both know that is no longer true
or maybe our connection was never there to
begin with.

It feels like something happened,
like a switch you don't want to admit.
I need to tell you I can't do this.

We can't just casually visit
after all the hurt you caused
after all the pain I've felt.

Now it's time
to say goodbye,
I wish you well.

Dad

I thought you loved me,
I thought you cared,
I thought you'd keep your promises
and you'd be there.

The guilt,
the pain,
the regret,
It's all the same.

Same excuses every time,
now you've stepped out of line.
Alcohol took you away from me
and the drugs destroyed you.
You said you'd leave those things behind,
but you lied.

You swore to love me again
and start brand new.
Now I'm just sitting here
wanting you,
dreaming,
hoping,
wishing,
waiting.

My heart's breaking
and so is yours.

Your words were left unspoken,
but I can see it in your eyes.
You love me too.

I can't trust you anymore.
I can't love you anymore.
You've ruined me
from the inside out.
Never will I be the same.
Never will I miss you again, never.
Forever I will love you, forever.

For the Love of Cat

I wish I could wrap up my love for you
and the joy I feel when you choose me to be
your foundation.
Your stripes and colors are vibrant as the sun
shines
when you greet me with morning kisses and
coos.
I stumble as you scurry underneath my feet
just to be near me.
You are begging to be held
but you're the one holding me.

I'm still here because of you.
I made it here because of you.

So I will spend the rest of my life loving you,
the grey tabby who stood tall in the window,
chosen by the runaway girl.
Consoled me through every thunderstorm,
every empty feeling and all the dark thoughts.
Early mornings and late nights at the bakery
just to remind me I'm alive and you love me.

I'm still here because of you.
I am me because of you.

The Fosters

I crumbled at the thought of losing you,
but now that you're gone
I've never felt more free.

The Diary

I was five and skipping on the sidewalk.
My foster mom picked me up and let me pick a
treat.
I chose a small diary with a lock and key,
its butterfly cover perfect for me.

A child desperate for love and so lonely,
often judged for her stories.
The way she spoke so casually about neglect and
crime,
it was hard for people to grasp at times.

The diary then became my best friend.
I confided since it couldn't talk back
or tell me I should stop talking about that.
It didn't tell me I was weird or strange.
I shared my true thoughts and embraced this
change.

I carried the diary with me when I left
to a new house across the state.
I wrote about our birds that froze to death
and the age gap between my mother and
stepfather
and celebrating October birthdays

and my siblings I never got to see.
I stopped writing when I realized I had no
privacy,
told me my own secrets and then mocked me.
I did nothing wrong but they made me feel so
much shame.
To let the diary be my safe space,
they took that away from me.

Over and over and over the years
I would go back to read the diary so dear to my
heart,
remembering that young girl
Five and skipping on the sidewalk.
The diary is the one piece of my childhood I can
look back on fondly,
my own experiences and perspective.
This is the only thing I have from before the
worst of life happened.
I no longer have it.
My childhood is sitting in an evidence box,
and he is sitting behind bars
and they all get to move on with their lives.
Everyone except for me and my diary.

The Decade

The only thing you ever taught me
is to make sure I choose someone
who chooses me back.

Perhaps

Perhaps if he had known
the love of a mother,
maybe then he could have shown me
the love I desperately needed.

My Last Lullaby

The rest of the world is sleeping
but I'm wide awake.
The silence is comforting
yet something I can no longer take.

What do you do in a world,
a place where you don't fit?
I seek help from those around me,
but the questions, they run from it.

I don't know when this happened,
when I started feeling so damn lost.
How do I turn my thoughts around
and if I don't, then what's the cost?

My life, my dreams, my so called friends,
the ones who stab me in the back.
You were the ones to walk away,
and I'm constantly getting attacked.

The ones who say they're always here
are the ones who hurt me the most.
It's time for me to run away,
maybe to an island or a coast.

Someplace where the sun is up
and never goes to sleep.
Somewhere warm and comfortable,
a new home just for me.

But I can't go.
They tell me I'm not alone.
Then why is no one here?
"Just get over it."
I can't.

Falling apart as I look in the mirror,
all I see is a mistake.
That's all I've ever been.
His eyes, her everything else.
When is enough, enough?
When is it too much?
I can't.

Life is pointless.
Completely and utterly hopeless,
never-ending and unbearable,
but we're here nonetheless.

I'm reaching out again,
only this time it's the last.
No one cares or understands
so this is goodbye to my past.

The past that eats me up inside
every goddamn lonely night.
It'll never get better than this,
so I'm giving up the fight.

I have to make a choice
between this life and the unknown.
What if what comes next is worse,
or what if it's nothing at all?

It's a choice I can't take back and that's why I'm
still here.
I think about my friends and family,
If they'd cry and hurt or care.
Or would they celebrate
for no longer having to deal with me?
Maybe they'd be better off.
I'm just the mistake
they were forced to make.

I'm not worth getting to know.
I'm forever the broken child
who steals food in the house and cares about
everyone too much.
"Oh, what a horrible child."
These thoughts are no longer mild.

The pain is getting deeper now,
it's cutting like a knife.

The blood is pouring down my arms,
I'm choosing to end my life.

I'm drowning in my own blood now,
it's no longer in my sorrows.
My body is growing weaker now,
but the rest of the world is still asleep.
The silence is comforting
and something I no longer have to take.

Her

"My daughter is dead,"
is what she would have said
if I had gone through with it that day.
If I had said the word "rape".
I would have explained
what he did
what he took.
But she didn't ask.
She didn't pry.
She just said "okay".

If I knew then what I know now,
I can see it all so clearly.

"My daughter is dead,"
is what she would have said
if I had taken her advice.
To die in a tub could have been nice.
"Don't forget that next time you're depressed."
"Don't cut your wrists,
but if you do, be sure you're in the tub.
It'll be easier for someone to clean the blood."

If I knew then what I know now,
I can see it all so clearly.

Him

I wonder what it must be like
to lose your mother and not be able to cry.
You proved yourself heartless a long time ago
and I just need you to know
for every moment you are truly alone with your
thoughts
I hope you think about everything and everyone
you've lost
and contemplate what your abuse costs.
No, really.
Take it all in for a moment.
What a waste.
How did the young boy at his mother's funeral
become you?
How did the charming young husband
become you?
How did the kinship foster dad
become you?

You paint yourself so highly
but you've never even picked up a brush.
You believe you've done everything right.
Every holiday screaming match,
every vacation temper tantrum,
everything in your control.

Now you're just alone and angry and old
and your mother would be ashamed of you.

You see, I don't want revenge.
I don't wish you harm or pain.
What I want is for you to understand the damage
you've caused.
To know the man I was supposed to look up to
became a man I despise.
To know when you walked me down the aisle,
I chose wrong.
I want you to realize what you've done
and to sit with those feelings of anger and
disgust
and to know you are alone in this world.
No one is on your side.

Everything you've lost is because of you.
All I want is for you to see exactly who you are
and to finish out the rest of your life feeling
empty and numb
in an empty house where abuse mimics love.

The Four

I waited a thousand days for this moment.
A couple decades, if I'm honest.
The four of you ready to stand by my side.
This is sentencing day,
this is the day my inner child speaks up.
Silenced for far too long,
this is the day my inner raging teen shouts from
the rooftops.

This happened and you are wrong.

I wish I could say I'm okay now
or I feel safer
or that it's over.
I'm not
and I don't
and it never will be.

But I fought for little me,
I broke the silence and shame she was forced to
carry.

If I knew then what I know now,
I can see it all so clearly.

They will never love me
but I know the four of you do.
You believed me,
never questioned or deceived,
loved me through the grief.
You are my safe people.
Four hands on my shoulder
during the longest hour of my life.
It all came crashing and we were all let down.
But I never would've made it this far
without the four of you.

You Closed the Door

I don't wanna fight this anymore.
They say when one door closes
another one will open,
but you slammed it shut,
then you lost the key
and swallowed it.
How can I do this?
I can't.
And at first, I thought maybe you'd wonder why
but then you didn't even try
to understand what I felt and everything I saw.
You walked away as if I meant nothing to you at
all.

Sincerely, the Monster

To you, I was just a number,
possibly the first but not the last.
To me, you were just my brother.
You dragged your hands across my body,
your weight pressed against me,
your fingers inside me.
To you, it was just another day.
To me, it was always the worst day.

Your eyes grew dark each time,
learning what you could get away with.
Even when you were caught
you kept going.
It was like a game to you.
You got off on breaking the rules.
To you, it was just a little fun.
To me, it made me want to run.

Mom

What if it hurts to let go
and it hurts to hold on?
What if it kills me knowing you're fine,
you've moved on
and without me, you're gone?

What if it hurts to think about saying goodbye?
Goodbye forever?
You'll never be mine.
Your selfish ways got the best of you and me.
I hope for your sake, someday you'll see.

What if we're better off
but can't move on without you?
What if we want to know the real stories
but can't stand the idea of hearing those too?

Your lies and accusations,
your stupid fixations.
One day you'll get it.
One day you'll understand.

In a world full of maybes, I wish you were a yes
but I guess not.
I can't keep doing this
so this is the end.

Life is a Storm

It isn't always on my mind
or at least not all the time,
but it is a part of me
that will never go away.
No matter how hard I try
to forget the pain,
it's still there.

It rarely strikes
but when it does, it comes with thunder.
It shakes me from the ground up,
destroying my core,
ripping me from the inside.
Even though on the surface I'm fine
my soul is the rain pouring down.
It can be seen from miles away.
It's ignored.

You're in a safe place.
You hide from the rain
and tell me there is no storm.
There's a hurricane inside of me,
inside of my mind,
my heart is being tossed around in the eye of the
storm.

My body is used and worn and damaged.

I have to heal myself somehow
but the storm never stops.
I have to heal without time to heal.
I have to mend without help to mend.
I'm still being tossed around.

This storm has been endless for nine years
and even though others could see the rain,
the storm still came.

My Knight

Sometimes I wake up and roll over,
pull you a little closer,
take a moment to remember how lucky I am
to have met you when I did.
Blue eyes and laughing on the floor,
pacific views and deeper feelings for you,
falling fast.
To be chosen by you.

Crunching leaves and 5 a.m. alarms,
late nights and hour-long drives,
You are my safety net.
Catch me and take me away from this place,
falling hard.
To be loved so effortlessly.

Handwritten love notes all over your house,
Stopping by for kisses whenever you're close.
You have my word,
You are mine, little bird.

My Rainbow

Somewhere in another universe
you are here with me
and here we are together.

Sometime in another life
I get to grow you,
hold you,
know you.

Someplace in a faraway land
your hand is holding mine,
you have my eyes,
and you are the love of my life.

Someday soon I'll get my rainbow
but I'll never stop missing you.